SELECT SERIES

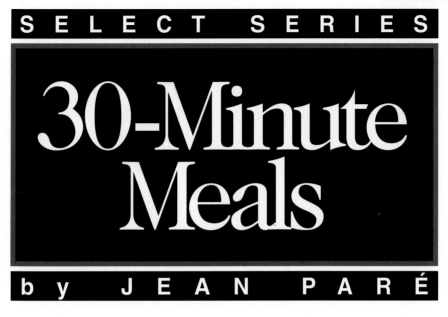

30-Minute Meals

by JEAN PARÉ

selected recipes from

Company's Coming

COOKBOOKS

30-Minute Meals

First printing February 1998

Canadian Cataloguing in Publication Data
Paré, Jean
    30-minute meals
Includes index.
Published also in French under title: Des repas en trente minutes
ISBN 1-896891-20-9
    1.Quick and easy cookery. I. Title.
II. Title: Thirty-minute meals.

TX833.5.P37 1998   641.5'55   C97-900800-X

Published simultaneously in
Canada and the United States of America by
The Recipe Factory Inc.
in conjunction with
Company's Coming Publishing Limited
2311 - 96 Street
Edmonton, Alberta, Canada T6N 1G3
Tel: 403 • 450-6223
Fax: 403 • 450-1857

COOKBOOKS

Company's Coming is a registered
trademark owned by
Company's Coming Publishing Limited

30-Minute Meals was created thanks to the dedicated efforts of the people and organizations listed below.

COMPANY'S COMING PUBLISHING LIMITED

Author	Jean Paré
President	Grant Lovig
V.P., Product Development	Kathy Knowles
Production Coordinator	Derrick Sorochan
Design	Nora Cserny
Typesetting	Marlene Crosbie
	Jaclyn Draker

THE RECIPE FACTORY INC.

Research & Development Manager	Nora Prokop
Test Kitchen Supervisor	Lynda Elsenheimer
Editor/Food Stylist	Stephanie With
Assistant Editor	Michelle White
Photographer	Stephe Tate Photo
Prop Stylist	Gabriele McEleney

Our special thanks to the following businesses for providing extensive props for photography.

Chintz & Company
Eaton's
Enchanted Kitchen
La Cache
Le Gnome
Scona Clayworks
Sears Canada
Stokes
The Bay
Tile Town Ltd.

Color separations, printing, and binding by Friesens, Altona, Manitoba, Canada
Printed in Canada

FRONT COVER
Clockwise from top right:
Meaty Chili, page 26
Smoked Salmon Pasta, page 47
Tacos, page 59
Chicken Stir-Fry, page 76

Table of Contents

The Jean Paré Story

Jean Paré grew up understanding that the combination of family, friends and home cooking is the essence of a good life. From her mother she learned to appreciate good cooking, while her father praised even her earliest attempts. When she left home she took with her many acquired family recipes, her love of cooking and her intriguing desire to read recipe books like novels!

In 1963, when her four children had all reached school age, Jean volunteered to cater to the 50th anniversary of the Vermilion School of Agriculture, now Lakeland College. Working out of her home, Jean prepared a dinner for over 1000 people which launched a flourishing catering operation that continued for over eighteen years. During that time she was provided with countless opportunities to test new ideas with immediate feedback—resulting in empty plates and contented customers! Whether preparing cocktail sandwiches for a house party or serving a hot meal for 1500 people, Jean Paré earned a reputation for good food, courteous service and reasonable prices.

"Why don't you write a cookbook?" Time and again, as requests for her recipes mounted, Jean was asked that question. Jean's response was to team up with her son, Grant Lovig, in the fall of 1980 to form Company's Coming Publishing Limited. April 14, 1981, marked the debut of "150 DELICIOUS SQUARES", the first Company's Coming cookbook in what soon would become Canada's most popular cookbook series. By 1995, sales had surpassed ten million cookbooks.

Jean Paré's operation has grown from the early days of working out of a spare bedroom in her home to operating a large and fully equipped test kitchen in Vermilion, Alberta, near the home she and her husband Larry built. Full-time staff has grown steadily to include marketing personnel located in major cities across Canada plus selected U.S. markets. Home Office is located in Edmonton, Alberta, where distribution, accounting and administration functions are headquartered in the company's own 20,000 square foot facility. Growth continues with the recent addition of the Recipe Factory, a 2700 square foot test kitchen and photography studio located in Edmonton.

Company's Coming cookbooks are now distributed throughout Canada and the United States plus numerous overseas markets, all under the guidance of Jean's daughter, Gail Lovig. The series is published in English and French, plus a Spanish language edition is available in Mexico. Familiar and trusted Company's Coming-style recipes are now available in a variety of formats in addition to the bestselling soft cover series.

Jean Paré's approach to cooking has always called for quick and easy recipes using everyday ingredients. She continues to gain new supporters by adhering to what she calls "the golden rule of cooking": never share a recipe you wouldn't use yourself. It's an approach that works—*ten million times over!*

Foreword

There is nothing more convenient for today's busy households than quick and easy meals that take less than 30 minutes to prepare.

Here are some timesaving tips to help you keep meal preparation convenient and simple. To begin with, take a look through some of these recipes and make note of the more common ingredients. By stocking up on these items you can ultimately save yourself the aggravation and hassle of last minute dashes to the nearest grocery store.

Consider also the possibility of doubling a recipe—or even preparing a second recipe that can keep for a day. Before you know it, you have the next night's meal already prepared! If serving leftovers doesn't sound appealing to your family, simply add some variety with a different side dish.

Another time-saver tip is to get the family involved—an extra pair of hands is certain to make your meal preparation go twice as quickly. Investing in a few cutting boards and sharp knives will also help to make tasks easier.

Ready for dinner? What about a hearty Vegetable Beef Soup with wholesome multi-grain bread, or loaded Teriyaki Chicken Burgers accompanied by freshly cut raw vegetables? A meat and veggie-packed Stir-Fry Meal provides ample nutrition, especially when served over pasta or rice. Oriental Pasta Salad for dinner can offer a unique and filling alternative to the usual fare of meat and potatoes.

Yes it is possible—busy schedules and delicious home-cooked meals can go together! Just follow the great recipes and tips in *30-Minute Meals* and dinner will be served in no time.

Polynesian Shrimp, page 12.

Casseroles that take only 30 minutes to prepare and cook? Absolutely! Make use of your microwave oven for even quicker results. Or try a simple throw-together in the frying pan or saucepan. Keep patty shells and crêpes in the freezer; prepare the filling while the crêpes are defrosting or while the patty shells are baking.

CRUSTLESS CRAB PIE

Slightly cakey in texture. Tasty.

Canned crabmeat, drained, membrane removed	4 oz.	113 g
Grated gouda cheese	1 cup	250 mL
Cream cheese, cubed	4 oz.	125 g
Large eggs	4	4
Milk	1½ cups	375 mL
Biscuit mix	1 cup	250 mL
Paprika	½ tsp.	2 mL
Salt	¾ tsp.	4 mL

Layer crab, gouda cheese and cream cheese in lightly greased 9 inch (22 cm) glass cake layer pan.

Combine remaining 5 ingredients in blender. Process for 1 to 2 minutes until smooth. Pour over contents in glass pan. Elevate on overturned saucer. Microwave, uncovered, on medium-high (70%) power for about 22 minutes until set, rotating dish ½ turn at half time if you don't have a turntable. Makes 6 servings.

ASPARAGUS SHRIMP BAKE

Colorful. A good combination. Use canned or fresh shrimp.

Canned asparagus spears, drained	10 oz.	284 mL
Butter or hard margarine	2 tbsp.	30 mL
Chopped onion	2 tbsp.	30 mL
Sliced fresh mushrooms	2 cups	500 mL
All-purpose flour	2 tbsp.	30 mL
Salt	½ tsp.	2 mL
Milk	1 cup	250 mL
Grated medium Cheddar cheese	½ cup	125 mL
Canned small shrimp, drained	2 x 4 oz.	2 x 113 g
(or 1½ cups, 375 mL, fresh cooked)		
Sherry (or alcohol-free sherry)	2 tbsp.	30 mL
Butter or hard margarine	2 tbsp.	30 mL
Grated medium Cheddar cheese	½ cup	125 mL
Dry bread crumbs	½ cup	125 mL

Arrange asparagus in greased 8 x 12 inch (20 x 30 cm) dish.

Combine first amount of butter, onion and mushrooms in 1 quart (1 L) casserole. Microwave, covered with waxed paper, on high (100%) power for about 5 minutes, stirring once or twice, until tender.

Mix in flour and salt. Stir in milk. Microwave, uncovered, on high (100%) power for about 4 minutes, stirring at half time, until mixture boils and thickens.

Add first amount of cheese, shrimp and sherry. Stir. Pour over asparagus.

Melt second amount of butter in small bowl, uncovered, on high (100%) power for about 35 seconds. Add second amount of cheese and bread crumbs. Stir. Sprinkle over top. Microwave, uncovered, on high (100%) power for 5 to 6 minutes until hot, rotating dish ½ turn at half time if you don't have a turntable. Cuts into 8 pieces.

Pictured on this page.

TUNA CASSEROLE

A chive biscuit topping covers sauced tuna and peas. Just add potatoes, noodles or rice for a complete meal.

Hard margarine (butter browns too fast)	¼ cup	60 mL
Chopped onion	¼ cup	60 mL
Chopped green pepper	2 tbsp.	30 mL
All-purpose flour	¼ cup	60 mL
Salt	½ tsp.	2 mL
Pepper	⅛ tsp.	0.5 mL
Milk	1½ cups	375 mL
Cooked peas (or half peas and half other cooked vegetable)	2 cups	500 mL
Canned tuna, drained and flaked	2 × 6½ oz.	2 × 184 g
CHIVE BISCUITS		
All-purpose flour	1 cup	250 mL
Baking powder	2 tsp.	10 mL
Chopped chives	1 tbsp.	15 mL
Salt	¼ tsp.	1 mL
Butter or hard margarine	3 tbsp.	50 mL
Milk	6 tbsp.	100 mL

Melt margarine in saucepan. Add onion and green pepper. Sauté until soft.

Mix in flour, salt and pepper. Stir in milk until mixture boils and thickens.

And peas and tuna. Stir. Pour into ungreased 2 quart (2 L) casserole.

Chive Biscuits: Measure flour, baking powder, chives and salt into bowl. Cut in butter until mixture is crumbly.

Add milk. Stir to form soft ball. Knead 5 or 6 times on lightly floured surface. Roll or pat to ½ inch (12 mm) thick. Cut with fish-shaped cookie cutter or into 2 inch (5 cm) rounds. Arrange over casserole. Bake, uncovered, in 425°F (220°C) oven for 20 to 25 minutes until biscuits are risen and browned. Makes 6 servings.

Pictured on page 9.

·PARÉ
  pointer

If anyone has to be

thrifty, let it be

ancestors.

Left: Tuna Bake, page 9. Right: Tuna Casserole, page 8.

TUNA BAKE

Another easy-to-make casserole.

Condensed cream of mushroom soup	**10 oz.**	**284 mL**
Water	**¼ cup**	**60 mL**
Chow mein noodles	**1 cup**	**250 mL**
Canned tuna, drained	**6½ oz.**	**184 g**
Thinly sliced celery	**1 cup**	**250 mL**
Chopped onion	**⅓ cup**	**75 mL**
Salted cashews	**½ cup**	**125 mL**
Chow mein noodles	**½ cup**	**125 mL**

Place first 7 ingredients in bowl. Stir and toss until well mixed. Spoon into greased 2 quart (2 L) casserole.

Sprinkle with second amount of noodles. Microwave, covered, on high (100%) power for 9 to 13 minutes until celery is cooked, rotating dish ½ turn at half time if you don't have a turntable. Makes 4 servings.

Pictured above.

CREAMED CHICKEN ON TOAST

You can make this from your shelf if you have chicken or turkey on hand. Liked by everyone.

Butter or hard margarine	**1 tbsp.**	**15 mL**
Chopped onion	**½ cup**	**125 mL**
Chopped celery	**¼ cup**	**60 mL**
All-purpose flour	**3 tbsp.**	**50 mL**
Condensed cream of mushroom soup	**10 oz.**	**284 mL**
Milk	**1¾ cups**	**425 mL**
Parsley flakes	**½ tsp.**	**2 mL**
Ground thyme	**⅛ tsp.**	**0.5 mL**
Salt	**½ tsp.**	**2 mL**
Pepper	**⅛ tsp.**	**0.5 mL**
Cooked chicken or turkey, cut up	**3 cups**	**750 mL**
Bread slices, toasted and buttered	**8**	**8**

Melt butter in heavy saucepan. Add onion and celery. Sauté until onion is soft and clear.

Sprinkle with flour. Mix well. Add next 6 ingredients. Stir until mixture boils and thickens. Add chicken and heat through.

Place 2 slices of toast on each plate. Divide creamed chicken on top. Serves 4.

·PARÉ
pointer

Gold soup is made

with fourteen carrots.

HAM CRÊPES

These crêpes contain not only ham but a rich mushroom sauce as well.

FILLING

Fresh mushrooms, sliced	**1½ lbs.**	**680 g**
Butter or hard margarine	**2-4 tbsp.**	**30-60 mL**
All-purpose flour	**1 tbsp.**	**15 mL**
Milk or cream	**½ cup**	**125 mL**

SAUCE

All-purpose flour	**1½ tbsp.**	**25 mL**
Butter or hard margarine	**1½ tbsp.**	**25 mL**
Salt	**¼ tsp.**	**1 mL**
Pepper, light sprinkle		
Milk or cream	**1 cup**	**250 mL**
Thin cooked ham slices	**12**	**12**
Prepared crêpes	**12**	**12**

Dill weed, sprinkle (or about 1 cup, 250 mL, grated Swiss cheese)

Filling: Sauté mushrooms in butter for about 5 minutes.

Sprinkle flour over mushrooms. Stir. Add milk. Stir to thicken. Cool.

Sauce: Mix flour into butter over medium heat. Add salt, pepper and milk. Stir until mixture boils and thickens.

Lay ham slices over crêpes. Spoon ¼ cup (60 mL) mushroom mixture over end of each ham slice. Roll and place in greased 9 x 13 inch (22 x 33 cm) baking dish. Pour sauce over all.

Sprinkle with dill weed or cheese. Bake, covered, in 400°F (205°C) oven for 15 minutes until hot. Serves 6.

Pictured on page 13.

POLYNESIAN SHRIMP

Surrounded by pineapple and green pepper with a rich looking sweet and sour sauce. Serve over rice or noodles. Freezes well.

Hard margarine (butter browns too fast)	1 tbsp.	15 mL
Green pepper, seeded and cut in slivers	1	1
Canned pineapple chunks, with juice	14 oz.	398 mL
Prepared orange juice	1/2 cup	125 mL
Lemon juice, fresh or bottled	1 tsp.	5 mL
Soy sauce	1 tbsp.	15 mL
Granulated sugar	1 tbsp.	15 mL
Salt	1/8 tsp.	0.5 mL
Cornstarch	1 tbsp.	15 mL
Water	2 tbsp.	30 mL
Medium shrimp, peeled and deveined	1 lb.	454 g
Boiling water, to cover		

Melt margarine in saucepan. Add green pepper. Sauté until tender crisp.

Add pineapple with juice, orange juice, lemon juice, soy sauce, sugar and salt. Bring to a boil.

Stir cornstarch and water together in small cup. Stir into boiling mixture until it returns to a boil and thickens. Keep warm.

Cook shrimp in boiling water for 3 to 5 minutes until pinkish and curled. Drain. Add to pineapple mixture. Stir. Serves 4.

Pictured on page 5 and on page 13.

PARÉ
pointer

A quick way to be

an actor is to break

a leg. You'll be in a

cast for months.

Clockwise from top right: Turkey Chow Mein, page 18; Ham Crêpes, page 11; and Polynesian Shrimp, page 12.

CHICKEN RICE CASSEROLE

Chicken and rice cook together. Worry free.

Instant rice	¾ cup	175 mL
Condensed cream of mushroom soup	10 oz.	284 mL
Milk	⅔ cup	150 mL
Chicken thighs, skin removed	8	8
Envelope dry onion soup mix (stir before dividing)	½ x 1½ oz.	½ x 42 g

Mix rice, soup and milk in bowl. Spread in 9 x 9 inch (22 x 22 cm) casserole.

Lay chicken over top around outside edges crowding to fit. Sprinkle with soup mix. Cover. Microwave on high (100%) power for about 25 minutes, rotating dish ½ turn every 5 minutes if you don't have a turntable, until chicken is tender. Let stand 15 minutes. Serves 4.

Pictured on this page.

TURKEY PIE

A regular feature after a turkey dinner.

Chopped cooked turkey	2 cups	500 mL
Condensed cream of mushroom soup	10 oz.	284 mL
Chopped celery, cooked	1 cup	250 mL
Milk	¾ cup	175 mL
Salt	½ tsp.	2 mL
Pepper	⅛ tsp.	0.5 mL
Biscuit mix	2 cups	500 mL
Milk, as directed on package	¾ cup	175 mL

Put turkey, soup and cooked celery in 1½ quart (1.5 L) casserole. Stir in milk, salt and pepper. Heat in 400°F (205°C) oven until bubbling hot.

Mix biscuit mix and milk as for dumplings. Drop by spoonful over top of hot meat and sauce. Bake in 450°F (230°C) oven for 15 minutes or until brown. Serves 4 to 6.

Pictured on page 25.

CHICKEN STROGANOFF

An ample amount of chicken, sauce and flavor. Serve over pasta, rice or fluffy mashed potatoes.

Boneless, skinless chicken breasts, halved	**3**	**3**
Medium onion, sliced	**1**	**1**
Butter or hard margarine	**1 tbsp.**	**15 mL**
Sliced fresh mushrooms	**1 cup**	**250 mL**
All-purpose flour	**1 tbsp.**	**15 mL**
Water	**¾ cup**	**175 mL**
Tomato paste	**3 tbsp.**	**50 mL**
Apple juice	**¼ cup**	**60 mL**
Chicken bouillon powder	**2 tsp.**	**10 mL**
Garlic powder	**¼ tsp.**	**1 mL**
Paprika	**¼ tsp.**	**1 mL**
Pepper	**⅛ tsp.**	**0.5 mL**
Sour cream	**⅔ cup**	**150 mL**

Cut chicken into thin strips. Arrange in 9 x 9 inch (22 x 22 cm) casserole. Cook in 2 batches for convenience. Cover. Microwave on high (100%) power for about 4 minutes, stirring at half time.

Place onion and butter in separate medium bowl. Cover. Microwave on high (100%) power for about 1 minute. Stir. Microwave, covered, on high (100%) power for about 3 minutes until almost cooked.

Stir in mushrooms. Cover. Microwave on high (100%) power for about 3 minutes.

Mix in flour. Stir in next 7 ingredients. Microwave, uncovered, on high (100%) for about 1 minute. Stir. Microwave on high (100%) power for 1 minute. Stir. Microwave, covered, on high (100%) power for about 3 minutes until mixture boils and thickens slightly.

Add chicken and sour cream. Stir. Microwave, covered, on high (100%) power for about 2 minutes until heated through but not boiling. Serves 4.

Pictured on this page.

FRANKFURTER STEW

Jazz up wieners with onion and tomatoes for a good flavor. Serve with crusty rolls.

Chunked, chopped or sliced onion	2 cups	500 mL
Green pepper, chopped	1	1
Butter or hard margarine	3 tbsp.	50 mL
All-purpose flour	2 tbsp.	30 mL
Canned stewed tomatoes	2 × 14 oz.	2 × 398 mL
Wieners (10 to 12), cut bite size	1 lb.	454 g
Granulated sugar	2 tsp.	10 mL
Salt	½ tsp.	2 mL
Pepper	¼ tsp.	1 mL

Sauté onion and green pepper in butter in frying pan until soft.

Mix in flour. Stir in tomatoes until mixture boils and thickens.

Add remaining 4 ingredients. Stir. Cover and simmer slowly to blend flavors and to heat through. Serves 4 to 5.

Pictured on this page.

CHILI

Excellent as chili but it also makes a good thick sauce for pasta.

Lean ground beef	1½ lbs.	680 g
Chopped onion	1 cup	250 mL
Chopped celery	½ cup	125 mL
Canned stewed tomatoes	14 oz.	398 mL
Canned kidney beans, with liquid	14 oz.	398 mL
Condensed tomato soup	10 oz.	284 mL
Chili powder	2 tsp.	10 mL
Granulated sugar	1 tsp.	5 mL
Garlic salt	¼ tsp.	1 mL
Ground oregano	⅛ tsp.	0.5 mL
Salt	½ tsp.	2 mL
Pepper	⅛ tsp.	0.5 mL

(continued on next page)

Mix ground beef, onion and celery in 3 quart (3 L) casserole. Cover with waxed paper. Microwave on high (100%) power for about 9 minutes, stirring every 3 minutes, until no pink remains in beef. Drain.

Add remaining 9 ingredients. Stir. Cover. Microwave on high (100%) power for about 9 minutes until mixture starts to boil. Microwave, uncovered, on medium (50%) power for about 15 minutes to blend flavors and thicken a bit. Makes 6¾ cups (1.7 L).

REUBEN CASSEROLE

A splendid dish. Contains cheese, tomato and the usual corned beef and sauerkraut.

Canned sauerkraut, drained	**14 oz.**	**398 mL**
Canned corned beef, crumbled	**12 oz.**	**340 g**
Grated medium Cheddar cheese	**1½ cups**	**375 mL**
Salad dressing (or mayonnaise)	**½ cup**	**125 mL**
Milk	**½ cup**	**125 mL**
Fresh tomatoes, diced	**2**	**2**
Onion powder	**¼ tsp.**	**1 mL**
Butter or hard margarine	**2 tbsp.**	**30 mL**
Dry bread crumbs	**½ cup**	**125 mL**
Grated medium Cheddar cheese	**½ cup**	**125 mL**
Paprika	**½ tsp.**	**2 mL**

Place sauerkraut in 2 quart (2 L) casserole. Spread corned beef over top. Sprinkle first amount of cheese over corned beef.

Whisk salad dressing and milk together. Stir in tomatoes and onion powder. Pour over cheese in casserole.

Microwave butter on high (100%) power in small bowl for about 20 seconds or until melted. Stir in bread crumbs, second amount of cheese and paprika. Sprinkle over tomatoes. Pat lightly. Cover with waxed paper. Microwave on medium-high (70%) power for about 12 minutes until bubbly hot, rotating dish ½ turn at half time if you don't have a turntable. Let stand 5 minutes. Serves 6.

Pictured on this page.

TURKEY CHOW MEIN

A colorful top-of-the-stove dish.

Instant rice	2½ cups	625 mL
Boiling water	2½ cups	625 mL
Canned mushrooms, whole or sliced, drained	10 oz.	284 mL
Canned sliced water chestnuts, drained	10 oz.	284 mL
Celery stalks, sliced thinly on angle	2	2
Chopped green pepper	¼ cup	60 mL
Chopped fresh green onion	⅓ cup	75 mL
Chopped pimiento, or strips	2 tbsp.	30 mL
Chopped cooked turkey	2 cups	500 mL
Thinly sliced onion	½ cup	125 mL
Butter or hard margarine	½ cup	125 mL
Large eggs, fork beaten	3	3
Salt	1½ tsp.	7 mL
Pepper	¼ tsp.	1 mL
Canned bean sprouts, with liquid	19 oz.	540 mL
Soy sauce	1 tbsp.	15 mL

Prepare rice with water according to package directions. Cool.

Combine mushrooms, water chestnuts, celery, green pepper, green onion, pimiento, turkey and onion in large bowl. Set aside.

Melt butter in frying pan. Add eggs, salt and pepper. Fry for a few minutes, stirring with fork to keep broken up. Do not allow eggs to become too firm. Add rice and turkey mixture. Stir to combine over low heat. Add a bit of water to simmer if too dry.

Stir in sprouts with liquid and soy sauce. Simmer, covered, for 10 to 15 minutes until hot. If too dry, add 2 tbsp. (30 mL) butter or hard margarine. Serves 8.

Pictured on page 13.

PARÉ
pointer

For their church

they want a bell that

will only sound off

when it's tolled.

SHRIMPY CHICKEN AND RICE

This combination is excellent over rice and equally good over noodles.

Long grain rice	1¹/₂ cups	375 mL
Boiling water	3 cups	750 mL
Salt (optional)	¹/₂ tsp.	2 mL
SHRIMP SAUCE		
Butter or hard margarine	¹/₄ cup	60 mL
Sliced fresh mushrooms	2 cups	500 mL
Finely chopped onion	3 tbsp.	50 mL
All-purpose flour	¹/₄ cup	60 mL
Skim evaporated milk	13¹/₂ oz.	385 mL
Milk	²/₃ cup	150 mL
Cooked shrimp (or 1 can 4 oz., 113 g, drained)	1 cup	250 mL
Coarsely chopped cooked chicken	2 cups	500 mL
Chopped chives	2 tbsp.	30 mL
Sherry (or alcohol-free sherry)	2 tbsp.	30 mL
Chopped pimiento	2 tbsp.	30 mL

Cook rice in boiling water and salt for about 15 minutes until rice is tender and water is absorbed.

Shrimp Sauce: Melt butter in frying pan. Add mushrooms and onion. Sauté until soft.

Mix in flour. Stir in both milks until mixture boils and thickens.

Add shrimp, chicken and chives. Stir. Heat through.

Stir in sherry and pimiento. Spoon over rice. Makes 4 cups (1 L).

Pictured on this page.

BEEF STROGANOFF

Whether company comes for dinner or for an evening, this is a festive dish to serve. Really rich-looking served over a bed of buttered noodles.

All-purpose flour	$\frac{1}{3}$ cup	75 mL
Salt	$\frac{1}{2}$ tsp.	2 mL
Pepper	$\frac{1}{8}$ tsp.	0.5 mL
Hard margarine (butter browns too fast)	2 tbsp.	30 mL
Filet or sirloin steak, cut in $\frac{1}{4}$ inch, 6 mm, strips	1 lb.	454 g
Thinly sliced fresh mushrooms	1 cup	250 mL
Medium onion, chopped	1	1
Garlic powder (or 1 clove, minced)	$\frac{1}{4}$ tsp.	1 mL
Butter or hard margarine	2 tbsp.	30 mL
Beef stock	$1\frac{1}{2}$ cups	375 mL
Tomato sauce	1 tbsp.	15 mL
Sour cream	1 cup	250 mL
Sherry (or alcohol-free sherry)	2 tbsp.	30 mL

Mix flour, salt and pepper in small bowl.

Melt margarine in frying pan. Dredge steak in flour mixture and put into pan. Brown quickly on both sides.

Add mushrooms, onion, garlic powder and butter. Simmer, stirring often, until onion is soft. Stir in remaining flour mixture.

Add beef stock and tomato sauce. Stir until mixture boils and thickens. Stir in sour cream and sherry. Heat through. Serves 4.

Pictured on page 25.

TIP

For quick cooked chicken, place boneless, skinless chicken breast halves in a shallow glass baking dish. Microwave on high (100%) power for 8 to 10 minutes or just until chicken is no longer pink. Rearrange chicken halfway through cooking. Cool. Cut into strips or cubes.

ROAST BEEF HASH

Leftover roast beef makes a good busy day meal.

Diced onion	**1 cup**	**250 mL**
Butter or hard margarine	**1 tbsp.**	**15 mL**
Medium potato	**1**	**1**
Leftover cooked roast beef, diced	**2 cups**	**500 mL**
Water	**⅓ cup**	**75 mL**
Beef bouillon powder	**1 tsp.**	**5 mL**
Salt	**½ tsp.**	**2 mL**
Pepper	**¼ tsp.**	**1 mL**

Place onion and butter in 2 cup (500 mL) container. Microwave on high (100%) power for about 30 seconds to melt butter. Stir. Cover. Microwave on high (100%) power for about 3 minutes until onion is soft.

Pierce potato in 3 or 4 spots. Microwave on high (100%) power for about 2 minutes. Turn potato over. Microwave on high (100%) power for about 2 minutes until tender. Peel and dice.

Combine onion, potato and remaining 5 ingredients in 2 quart (2 L) casserole. Stir. Cover. Microwave on high (100%) power for about 4 minutes, stirring once or twice, until piping hot. Makes 3 cups (750 mL).

Pictured above.

FAJITAS

For a real fun meal, try fa-HEE-tahs. Serve with or without peppers.

Cooking oil	1 tbsp.	15 mL
Boneless, skinless chicken breast halves, sliced in long thin strips	4	4
Spanish onion, sliced in rings	1	1
Green pepper, cut in strips (see Note)	1	1
Red pepper, cut in strips (see Note)	1	1
Salt, sprinkle		
Pepper, sprinkle		
Lemon juice, fresh or bottled	1 tbsp.	15 mL
Flour tortillas, 7 inch (17.5 cm), heated in covered bowl	8-10	8-10
Grated medium or sharp Cheddar cheese	1 cup	250 mL
Sour cream	1 cup	250 mL
Salsa (mild or medium)	1 cup	250 mL
Guacamole	1 cup	250 mL

Heat cooking oil in frying pan. Add chicken. Stir-fry until no pink remains. Turn into bowl.

To same frying pan, add onion, peppers and more cooking oil if needed. Sauté until soft and browned. Spread on warm platter.

Return chicken to pan to heat. Sprinkle with salt and pepper. Drizzle with lemon juice. Heat quickly. Place over onion mixture.

To prepare for eating, lay 1 tortilla on plate. Place some onion mixture down center, then a few chicken strips on top. Garnish with cheese, sour cream, salsa and guacamole. Roll. Fold up and hold one end while you bite from the other end. Makes 8 to 10 fajitas.

Note: To make without peppers, use 2 onions.

Pictured on this page.

CHICKEN IN THE SHELL

Puff pastry shells overflowing with chicken sauce. Good on toast too.

Patty shells (puff pastry shells)	**8**	**8**
FILLING		
Butter or hard margarine	¼ cup	60 mL
Grated carrot	½ cup	125 mL
All-purpose flour	¼ cup	60 mL
Chicken bouillon powder	2 tsp.	10 mL
Onion powder	¼ tsp.	1 mL
Salt	1 tsp.	5 mL
Pepper	⅛ tsp.	0.5 mL
Milk	3 cups	750 mL
Chopped cooked chicken	2 cups	500 mL
Canned sliced mushrooms, drained	10 oz.	284 mL
Chopped pimiento	2 tbsp.	30 mL

Bake patty shells according to package directions.

Filling: Melt butter in large saucepan. Add carrot. Sauté until soft. Do not brown.

Sprinkle flour, bouillon powder, onion powder, salt and pepper over carrot. Mix in. Add milk stirring until mixture boils and thickens.

Add chicken, mushrooms and pimiento. Heat through. Spoon into and over patty shells. Filling freezes well. Serves 4.

Pictured on this page.

SLOPPY JOES

If you want to be prepared for sixteen people, simply multiply this by four. Freezing leftovers couldn't be easier.

Cooking oil	1 tbsp.	15 mL
Ground beef	1 lb.	454 g
Chopped onion	1 cup	250 mL
Chopped green pepper (optional)	2 tbsp.	30 mL
All-purpose flour	2 tbsp.	30 mL
Tomato sauce	7½ oz.	213 mL
Water	1⅓ cups	325 mL
Worcestershire sauce	1½ tsp.	7 mL
White vinegar	1½ tsp.	7 mL
Brown sugar, packed	1½ tsp.	7 mL
Salt	1 tsp.	5 mL
Pepper	¼ tsp.	1 mL
Prepared mustard	¼ tsp.	1 mL
Hamburger buns, halved, and toasted (see Note)	4	4

Heat cooking oil in frying pan. Scramble-fry ground beef, onion and green pepper until onion is soft and beef is no longer pink.

Sprinkle with flour and mix well. Stir in tomato sauce and water until mixture boils and thickens. Turn into large heavy saucepan.

Add next 6 ingredients. Stir. Simmer gently, uncovered, stirring often for 10 to 15 minutes. Add more water if too thick.

Butter bun halves if desired. Spoon meat mixture over 2 bun halves on each plate. Freezes well. Serves 4.

Note: Hamburger buns may be toasted by placing cut side down in hot frying pan until browned or may be broiled cut side up.

Pictured on page 25.

Clockwise from top left: Turkey Pie, page 14;
Sloppy Joes, page 24; and Beef Stroganoff, page 20.

MEATY CHILI

Just use what you need and freeze the rest. Double recipe to feed sixteen. Contains vegetables.

Butter or hard margarine	2 tbsp.	30 mL
Chopped onion	1 cup	250 mL
Green pepper, chopped	1	1
Lean ground beef	2½ lbs.	1.14 kg
Sliced mushrooms, drained	10 oz.	284 mL
Kidney beans, drained	2 × 14 oz.	2 × 398 mL
Kernel corn	12 oz.	341 mL
Tomato sauce	3 × 7½ oz.	3 × 213 mL
Chili powder	1 tbsp.	15 mL
Granulated sugar	1 tbsp.	15 mL
Garlic salt	¼ tsp.	1 mL
Salt	2 tsp.	10 mL
Pepper	¼ tsp.	1 mL
Peas, fresh or frozen	2 cups	500 mL

Melt butter in large, heavy saucepan. Add onion and green pepper. Sauté until onion is clear and soft.

Add ground beef. Stir to break up. Brown beef until no longer pink. Transfer to large saucepan.

Add next 9 ingredients to saucepan. Bring to a boil. Simmer, covered, for 15 minutes.

Add peas. Simmer for about 5 minutes. Serves 8.

Pictured on front cover.

PARÉ
pointer

The story about

the peacock is a

beautiful tale.

Do you sometimes feel like just having a salad for lunch or dinner? These main dish salads contain many ingredients that will give you the protein, carbohydrates, vitamins and minerals that make up a full meal. Enjoy a cold, refreshing yet filling salad on a warm summer day.

CHEF'S SALAD

A meal in itself when accompanied by crusty rolls. Serve with your favorite dressing.

Medium head iceberg lettuce (see Note)	1	1
Red onion, sliced (optional)	1	1
Cucumber, peeled or scored and diced	½	½
Green onions, sliced	4	4
Edam cheese (or Swiss) strips	1 cup	250 mL
Cooked chicken or turkey strips	1 cup	250 mL
Ham strips	1 cup	250 mL
Thinly sliced radish (optional)	½ cup	125 mL
Tomatoes, cut into lengthwise wedges	2	2
Large hard-boiled eggs, cut into lengthwise wedges	3	3

Tear or cut lettuce into large bowl or 6 single serving bowls.

Add next 7 ingredients to lettuce being sure to save enough of each item for garnish. Toss together. Arrange remainder over top of salad in attractive design.

Garnish with tomato wedges and hard cooked egg wedges. Serves 6.

Note: Adding half romaine lettuce or other greens gives more interest to the salad.

Pictured on page 31.

NIÇOISE SALAD

This main dish salad can be arranged to suit your fancy.

Small firm head iceberg lettuce, torn	1	1
Head romaine lettuce, torn	1	1
Canned tuna, drained	2 x 6½ oz.	2 x 184 g
Red onion, thinly sliced	1	1
Sliced black pitted olives	½ cup	125 mL
Thinly sliced celery	1 cup	250 mL
Medium potatoes, cooked and sliced	4	4
Canned French-cut green beans, drained	14 oz.	398 mL
Cooking oil	½ cup	125 mL
Red wine vinegar	3 tbsp.	50 mL
Chopped fresh parsley	¼ cup	60 mL
Lemon juice, fresh or bottled	1 tbsp.	15 mL
Garlic powder	¼ tsp.	1 mL
Salt	½ tsp.	2 mL
Pepper	¼ tsp.	1 mL
Tomatoes, cut in lengthwise wedges	2	2
Hard-boiled eggs, quartered lengthwise	3	3
Anchovies, for garnish (optional)	6-12	6-12

Line large platter or salad bowl with lettuce.

Layer tuna, onion, olives, celery, potatoes and beans over top.

Mix cooking oil, vinegar, parsley, lemon juice, garlic powder, salt and pepper. Drizzle over salad.

Arrange tomato and egg wedges over or around salad. Make pattern with anchovies on top. Serves 6.

Pictured on page 33.

PARÉ
pointer

If you have a pig,

a pool table and a

tall tree, you have

a pork-cue-pine.

COBB SALAD

A contribution to the salad world from California. Try your flair for arranging vegetables. Not as complicated as it looks.

DRESSING		
White vinegar	1/3 cup	75 mL
Cooking oil	2/3 cup	150 mL
Dry mustard powder	1/2 tsp.	2 mL
Granulated sugar	1/2 tsp.	2 mL
Garlic powder	1/8 tsp.	0.5 mL
Salt	1 tsp.	5 mL
Pepper	1/4 tsp.	1 mL
Blue cheese, crumbled (see Note)	1/4 cup	60 mL
SALAD		
Medium head iceberg lettuce, shredded	1	1
Watercress, cut up, stems removed	1 cup	250 mL
Hard-boiled eggs	3	3
Green onions, sliced	4	4
Bacon slices, cooked and crumbled	8	8
Cubed cooked chicken	2 1/2 cups	625 mL
Large tomato, finely chopped	1	1
Avocado, diced small	1	1

Dressing: Combine all 8 ingredients in bowl. Mix well.

Salad: Combine lettuce and watercress in large salad bowl. Add about 1/4 dressing. Toss to coat.

Remove yolks from eggs. Grate yolks. Grate whites separately. Arrange grated yolks in center of bowl, and surround with whites. Make separate wedges of onions, bacon, chicken, tomato and avocado or mix these five and pile around egg center. Serve with rest of dressing. Serves 4 to 6.

Note: You may prefer to make a wedge of crumbled blue cheese rather than add it to the dressing. You could also serve the lettuce on the side.

Pictured on this page.

TIP

To make a tortilla bowl, grease the outside of a 2 cup (500 mL) or 4 cup (1 L) glass liquid measure with no-stick cooking spray. Turn it upside down. Centre the tortilla over the bottom and press down and around to shape. Edges will be "wavy" Microwave on high (100%) power at 1 minute intervals until brown spots begin to appear on the surface of the tortilla. Cool then gently lift tortilla off the cup and turn over, keeping shape.

ORIENTAL PASTA SALAD

Fantastic flavor with or without shrimp.

Medium egg noodles	8 oz.	250 g
Boiling water	2½ qts.	2.5 L
Cooking oil (optional)	1 tbsp.	15 mL
Salt	2 tsp.	10 mL
Sliced fresh mushrooms	1 cup	250 mL
Green onions, chopped	2-3	2-3
Bean sprouts, large handful	1	1
Grated cabbage	1 cup	250 mL
Sliced cucumber, peeled or not	1 cup	250 mL
Sliced radishes	½ cup	125 mL
Grated carrot	¼ cup	60 mL
Small cooked fresh shrimp (or 1 can, 4 oz., 113 g), optional	1 cup	250 mL
DRESSING		
Hot water	2 tbsp.	30 mL
Chicken bouillon powder	1 tbsp.	15 mL
Soy sauce	3 tbsp.	50 mL
White vinegar	3 tbsp.	50 mL
Cooking oil	¼ cup	60 mL
Granulated sugar	2 tsp.	10 mL
Salt	½ tsp.	2 mL
Pepper	⅛ tsp.	0.5 mL

Cook noodles in boiling water, cooking oil and salt in uncovered Dutch oven for 5 to 7 minutes until tender but firm. Drain. Rinse with cold water. Drain well. Return noodles to Dutch oven.

Combine next 8 ingredients with noodles.

Dressing: Mix hot water with bouillon powder in small bowl. Add remaining 6 ingredients. Whisk well. Pour over noodle mixture.Toss. Put into bowl. Serves 8 as a main course.

Pictured on page 33.

POLYNESIAN CHICKEN SALAD

A wonderful meaty sauce spooned hot over lettuce. Different and so good.

Cooking oil	2 tbsp.	30 mL
Boneless, skinless chicken breast, halved, cut bite size	1	1
Boneless, skinless chicken thighs, cut bite size	4	4
Thinly sliced celery	1 cup	250 mL
Green onions, sliced	6	6
Canned bamboo shoots, drained	10 oz.	284 mL
Canned sliced mushrooms, drained	10 oz.	284 mL
Medium tomatoes, cubed	2	2
Soy sauce	3 tbsp.	50 mL
Ground ginger	1/8 tsp.	0.5 mL
Garlic powder	1/8 tsp.	0.5 mL
Salt	1/4 tsp.	1 mL
Cut or torn iceberg lettuce	6 cups	1.5 L

Heat cooking oil in wok or frying pan. Add chicken and celery. Sauté until no pink remains in chicken.

Add next 8 ingredients. Stir-fry for about 2 minutes.

Divide lettuce among 6 plates. Spoon hot mixture over top. Makes 6 servings.

Pictured below.

Left: Polynesian Chicken Salad, page 31. Right: Chef's Salad, page 27.

CHICKEN GREENS SALAD

Dressed with a piquant oil and vinegar dressing.

Boneless, skinless chicken breasts, halved	4	4
Cooking oil	1 tbsp.	15 mL
Torn or chopped romaine lettuce	6 cups	1.5 L
Medium tomatoes, diced	3	3
Green onions, chopped	4	4
Medium zucchini, slivered	2	2
HOUSE DRESSING		
Cooking oil	¼ cup	60 mL
White vinegar	2 tbsp.	30 mL
Granulated sugar	½ tsp.	2 mL
Salt	¼ tsp.	1 mL
Prepared mustard	½ tsp.	2 mL
Garlic powder	⅛ tsp.	0.5 mL
Pepper, light sprinkle		
Grated Parmesan cheese	1 tbsp.	15 mL

Brown chicken on both sides in cooking oil in frying pan. Continue to cook until no pink remains.

Toss next 4 ingredients together in large bowl.

House Dressing: Stir all ingredients together well in small bowl. Pour over salad. Toss to coat. Divide among 8 salad plates. Top with warm chicken. It looks better to cut chicken into ½ inch (12 mm) slices before placing over salad. Serves 8.

Pictured on page 33 and on page 80.

Clockwise from top right: Oriental Pasta Salad, page 30; Niçoise Salad, page 28; and Chicken Greens Salad, page 32.

CRAB LOUIS

A lunch in itself when accompanied by a dinner roll.

LOUIS DRESSING

Salad dressing (or mayonnaise)	½ cup	125 mL
Chili sauce	¼ cup	60 mL
Dry onion flakes	1 tsp.	5 mL
Milk or light cream	1 tbsp.	15 mL
Commercial French dressing	2 tbsp.	30 mL
Worcestershire sauce	½ tsp.	2 mL

SALAD

Small firm head iceberg lettuce	1	1
Canned crabmeat, drained, (or 2 cups, 500 mL, fresh) membrane removed	2 × 4 oz.	2 × 113 g
Hard-boiled eggs	4	4
Tomatoes	2	2

Louis Dressing: Mix all 6 ingredients in small bowl. Set aside.

Salad: Cut or tear lettuce. Pile in center of individual salad plates or in center of platter. Put crabmeat over top of lettuce, tossing it together a bit. Cut eggs lengthwise into quarters. Arrange around outside edge of lettuce. Cut tomatoes in wedges. Arrange around outside edge of lettuce also. Spoon some of the dressing over the lettuce-crab combination. Serve rest of dressing in separate bowl. Serves 4 to 6.

Pictured on this page.

Variation: Omit the Worcestershire sauce and French dressing. It is a bit milder and a pretty pink color.

SHRIMP LOUIS: Omit crab. Add same amount of shrimp, fresh or canned.

PASTA SALAD

Broccoli and grated cheese cheer up this salad with green and gold.

Elbow macaroni, or other small pasta	2 cups	500 mL
Boiling water	3 qts.	3 L
Cooking oil (optional)	1 tbsp.	15 mL
Salt	2 tsp.	10 mL
Broccoli, cut bite size	3 cups	750 mL
Sliced green onion	3 tbsp.	50 mL
Grated medium or sharp Cheddar cheese	1 cup	250 mL
Grated Monterey Jack cheese	1 cup	250 mL
Sliced fresh mushrooms	1 cup	250 mL
Toasted sesame seeds	3 tbsp.	50 mL
DRESSING		
Red wine vinegar	¼ cup	60 mL
Prepared mustard	4 tsp.	20 mL
Liquid honey	4 tsp.	20 mL
Soy sauce	1 tsp.	5 mL

Cook pasta in boiling water, cooking oil and salt in uncovered Dutch oven for 6 to 8 minutes until tender but firm. Drain. Rinse in cold water. Drain again well. Put into large bowl.

Add next 6 ingredients. Stir lightly.

Dressing: Mix all 4 ingredients well in small bowl. Pour over salad. Toss to mix. Makes 8 cups (2 L).

Pictured on this page.

These pasta recipes offer a variety of simple but creative options to choose from for every day of the week. Enjoy pasta with a seafood or chicken sauce or try a simple meat or tomato sauce. Be creative by substituting different pasta shapes. Whatever the occasion, pasta is a perfect choice.

PASTA KRAUT

Add a green salad and you have a great meal.

Lean ground beef	1½ lbs.	680 g
Chopped onion	1 cup	250 mL
Cooking oil	2 tbsp.	30 mL
Condensed cream of mushroom soup	10 oz.	284 mL
Canned sauerkraut, drained	14 oz.	398 mL
Salt	1 tsp.	5 mL
Pepper	¼ tsp.	1 mL
Wide egg noodles	8 oz.	250 g
Boiling water	2½ qts.	2.5 L
Cooking oil (optional)	1 tbsp.	15 mL
Salt	2 tsp.	10 mL

Scramble-fry ground beef and onion in first amount of cooking oil in large saucepan until onion is soft and beef is no longer pink.

Add soup, sauerkraut, first amount of salt and pepper.

Cook noodles in boiling water, second amounts of cooking oil and salt in uncovered Dutch oven for 5 to 7 minutes until tender but firm. Drain. Combine with beef mixture. Serves 6.

SAUCED PASTA

A creamy egg and asparagus sauce tops the pasta. Adds a wonderful flavor.

Fusilli or other spiral or tube pasta	4 cups	1 L
Boiling water	3 qts.	3 L
Cooking oil	1 tbsp.	15 mL
Salt	1 tbsp.	15 mL
SAUCE		
All-purpose flour	6 tbsp.	100 mL
Salt	1 tsp.	5 mL
Pepper	1/4 tsp.	1 mL
Onion powder	1/4 tsp.	1 mL
Skim evaporated milk	1 1/2 cups	375 mL
Milk	1 1/2 cups	375 mL
Butter or hard margarine	1 tbsp.	15 mL
Hard-boiled eggs, cut lengthwise into 8 thin wedges	2-4	2-4
Canned asparagus pieces, drained	12 oz.	341 mL

Cook pasta in boiling water, cooking oil and salt in uncovered Dutch oven for 10 to 12 minutes until tender but firm. Drain.

Sauce: Stir flour, salt, pepper and onion powder together in saucepan. Gradually stir in evaporated milk, ensuring there are no lumps. Stir in remaining milk. Heat and stir until sauce boils and thickens.

Stir in butter.

Add eggs and asparagus. Heat, stirring gently, until hot. Divide pasta among 4 plates. Spoon sauce over each. Serves 4.

Pictured on this page.

ALL-IN-ONE MACARONI

Talk about easy! The pasta is added uncooked.

Lean ground beef	1 lb.	454 g
Chopped onion	½ cup	125 mL
Garlic clove, minced	1	1
Cooking oil	1 tbsp.	15 mL
Canned tomatoes, with juice, mashed	14 oz.	398 mL
Water	1½ cups	375 mL
Soy sauce	1 tbsp.	15 mL
Dried sweet basil	⅛ tsp.	0.5 mL
Ground thyme	⅛ tsp.	0.5 mL
Elbow macaroni	2 cups	500 mL
Salt	1 tsp.	5 mL
Pepper	⅛ tsp.	0.5 mL
Granulated sugar	½ tsp.	2 mL

Scramble-fry ground beef, onion and garlic in cooking oil in Dutch oven or large saucepan until onion is soft and beef is no longer pink.

Add remaining 9 ingredients. Bring to a boil. Cover and simmer for about 15 minutes, stirring occasionally, until pasta is tender but firm. Serves 4.

FETTUCCINI

Quick to prepare. Red pepper and peas add color.

Fettuccini	1 lb.	454 g
Boiling water	4 qts.	4 L
Hard margarine (butter browns too fast)	2 tbsp.	30 mL
Frozen peas, thawed	1½ cups	375 mL
Red pepper, slivered	1	1
All-purpose flour	2 tbsp.	30 mL
Skim milk	1 cup	250 mL
Grated Parmesan cheese	6 tbsp.	100 mL

(continued on next page)

PARÉ
pointer

Old mathematicians

finally die when

their numbers are up.

Cook pasta in boiling water in uncovered Dutch oven for 9 to 11 minutes until tender but firm. Drain. Return pasta to Dutch oven.

Melt margarine in frying pan. Add peas and red pepper. Sauté for about 4 minutes until tender.

Sprinkle with flour. Mix. Stir in skim milk until mixture boils. Pour over drained pasta. Divide among 6 plates.

Sprinkle each plate with Parmesan cheese. Makes 9 cups (2.25 L). Serves 6.

Pictured on this page.

TUNA AND PASTA

Creamy and saucy with tomato added. Good.

Rotini, or other spiral or tube pasta	8 oz.	250 g
Boiling water	2½ qts.	2.5 L
Cooking oil (optional)	1 tbsp.	15 mL
Salt	2 tsp.	10 mL
Butter or hard margarine	2 tbsp.	30 mL
All-purpose flour	2 tbsp.	30 mL
Milk	1 cup	250 mL
Canned tomatoes, with juice, broken up	1 cup	250 mL
Salt	½ tsp.	2 mL
Dried oregano	1½ tsp.	7 mL
Canned tuna, drained	6½ oz.	184 g
Grated medium Cheddar cheese	1 cup	250 mL

Cook pasta in boiling water, cooking oil and first amount of salt in uncovered Dutch oven for 10 to 13 minutes until tender but firm. Drain.

Melt butter in large saucepan. Mix in flour. Add milk. Stir until mixture boils and thickens.

Add remaining 5 ingredients. Add pasta. Mix and heat through. Makes a generous 4 cups (1 L).

FETTUCCINI WITH TOMATO

What better combination than bacon and tomato.

Bacon slices, diced	8	8
Chopped onion	1½ cups	375 mL
Tomatoes, peeled, seeded and chopped (see Note)	4	4
Chopped fresh parsley	¼ cup	60 mL
Dried sweet basil	1 tsp.	5 mL
Garlic powder	½ tsp.	2 mL
Fettuccini	1 lb.	454 g
Boiling water	4 qts.	4 L
Cooking oil (optional)	1 tbsp.	15 mL
Salt	1 tbsp.	15 mL
Butter or hard margarine, melted	¼ cup	60 mL
Salt	1 tsp.	5 mL
Pepper	⅛ tsp.	0.5 mL

Grated Parmesan cheese, for garnish

Sauté bacon and onion in frying pan until onion is soft and clear.

Add tomato, parsley, basil and garlic powder. Stir and heat through. Keep warm.

Cook pasta in boiling water, cooking oil and first amount of salt in uncovered Dutch oven for about 9 to 11 minutes, until tender but firm. Drain. Return to Dutch oven.

Add butter, second amount of salt and pepper to pasta. Toss. Add tomato mixture. Toss. Taste for salt and pepper, adding more if needed.

Sprinkle with, or pass, Parmesan cheese on the side. Makes about 8 cups (2 L).

Note: To peel tomatoes, immerse in boiling water about about one minute or until skins will peel easily.

Pictured on this page.

TURKEY CASSEROLE

A tasty dish with broccoli and pasta.

Spaghetti, broken up	**7 oz.**	**196 g**
Boiling water	**6 cups**	**1.5 L**
Butter or hard margarine	**2 tbsp.**	**30 mL**
Frozen chopped broccoli	**10 oz.**	**284 g**
Process cheese spread (such as CheezWhiz)	**1 cup**	**250 mL**
Milk	**¹/₂ cup**	**125 mL**
Canned mushroom pieces, drained	**10 oz.**	**284 mL**
Chopped cooked turkey	**1 cup**	**250 mL**
Chopped pimiento	**2 tbsp.**	**30 mL**
Poultry seasoning	**¹/₄ tsp.**	**1 mL**
Onion salt	**¹/₄ tsp.**	**1 mL**

Place pasta and boiling water in deep 3 quart (3 L) bowl. Microwave, uncovered, on high (100%) power for about 7 minutes until it boils. Microwave on medium (50%) power for about 5 minutes until tender but firm. Drain. Return pasta to bowl.

Add butter. Toss.

Microwave broccoli, covered, in 1 quart (1 L) casserole on high (100%) power for about 6 minutes until tender. Drain well. Add to pasta.

Stir cheese and milk together in 2 cup (500 mL) measuring cup. Microwave 1¹/₂ minutes on high (100%) power, stirring every 30 seconds. Add to pasta. Stir.

Add remaining 5 ingredients to pasta. Stir. Turn into 2 quart (2 L) casserole. Cover. Microwave on high (100%) power for about 6 minutes until very hot, rotating dish ¹/₂ turn at half time if you don't have a turntable. Serves 4.

Variation: Chicken may be used instead of turkey.

TIP

Salting the water when boiling pasta adds flavor to the noodles, but is not necessary. For a change, use ¹/₂ to 1 tsp. (2 to 5 mL) dried sweet basil or garlic salt in place of the salt.

SPAGHETTI AND MEAT SAUCE

Creamy white noodles covered with a thick dark sauce and topped with Parmesan cheese.

Spaghetti	8 oz.	250 g
Boiling water	2½ qts.	2.5 L
Cooking oil (optional)	1 tbsp.	15 mL
Salt	2 tsp.	10 mL
SPAGHETTI MEAT SAUCE		
Lean ground beef	1½ lbs.	680 g
Finely chopped onion	½ cup	125 mL
Cooking oil	1 tbsp.	15 mL
Tomato sauce	7½ oz.	213 mL
Tomato paste	5½ oz.	156 mL
Sliced mushrooms, with liquid	10 oz.	284 mL
Envelope dry onion soup mix	1 x 1½ oz.	1 x 42 g
Parsley flakes	2 tsp.	10 mL

Grated Parmesan cheese, sprinkle

Cook pasta in boiling water, cooking oil and salt in uncovered Dutch oven for 11 to 13 minutes, until tender but firm.

Spaghetti Meat Sauce: Scramble-fry ground beef and onion in cooking oil in frying pan until beef is no longer pink and onion is soft.

Combine tomato sauce, tomato paste, mushrooms with liquid, onion soup mix and parsley flakes in large saucepan. Add beef mixture. Cover. Simmer for 5 minutes. Stir occasionally. This makes about 4½ cups (1.1 L) sauce.

Drain pasta and divide among 4 warm plates. Spoon meat sauce over top. Sprinkle with Parmesan cheese. Serves 4.

Clockwise from top right: Chicken Tetrazzini, page 49; Pasta Primavera, page 44; and Linguini with Red Clam Sauce, page 46.

PASTA PRIMAVERA

A huge, colorful mixture of pasta and vegetables. Makes a great meal.

Coarsely chopped broccoli	6 cups	1.5 L
Zucchini, cut in thin fingers	3 cups	750 mL
Frozen peas	2 cups	500 mL
Boiling water		
Salt	1 tsp.	5 mL
Cooking oil	1 tbsp.	15 mL
Garlic clove, minced	1	1
Sliced fresh mushrooms	2 cups	500 mL
Canned tomatoes, drained and broken up	14 oz.	398 mL
Chopped fresh parsley	¼ cup	60 mL
PASTA		
Linguini, or other noodle pasta	1 lb.	454 g
Boiling water	4 qts.	4 L
Cooking oil (optional)	1 tbsp.	15 mL
Salt	1 tbsp.	15 mL
Skim evaporated milk	13½ oz.	385 mL
Grated Parmesan cheese	½ cup	125 mL
Salt	1 tsp.	5 mL

Grated Parmesan cheese, sprinkle

· P A R É
pointer

He who says he is

too old to learn

anything new

probably always was.

Cook broccoli, zucchini and peas in boiling water and salt in saucepan for 3 minutes until tender crisp. Drain. Set aside.

Heat cooking oil in wok or frying pan. Add garlic and mushrooms. Sauté until soft and moisture has evaporated.

Add tomatoes and parsley. Sauté for 1 minute. Remove from heat.

Pasta: Cook pasta in boiling water, cooking oil and salt in uncovered Dutch oven for 9 to 11 minutes until tender but firm. Drain. Add to wok. Add vegetables.

(continued on next page)

Add milk, first amount of Parmesan cheese and salt. Heat and stir until mixture simmers. Simmer for about 3 minutes until mixture thickens slightly. Turn into large bowl.

Sprinkle with second amount of Parmesan cheese. Makes 13 cups (3.25 L).

Pictured on page 43.

CORNED PASTA

This colorful dish is easy to prepare. Pasta is added raw. Kernel corn adds to both taste and color.

Olive oil (or cooking oil)	1 tbsp.	15 mL
Lean ground beef	1 lb.	454 g
Chopped onion	2 cups	500 mL
Small green pepper, chopped	1	1
Canned tomatoes, with juice, mashed	28 oz.	796 mL
Canned kernel corn, drained	12 oz.	341mL
Water	3/4 cup	175 mL
Wagon wheel pasta, uncooked	8 oz.	250 g
Salt	1 tsp.	5 mL
Pepper	1/4 tsp.	1 mL
Garlic powder	1/4 tsp.	1 mL
Sliced black olives (optional)	1/4 cup	60 mL
Grated medium Cheddar cheese	1 cup	250 mL

Heat olive oil in large saucepan. Add ground beef, onion and green pepper. Scramble-fry until onion is soft and beef is no longer pink.

Add next 8 ingredients to beef mixture. Mix. Cover. Simmer gently for about 8 minutes until pasta is tender but firm. Stir occasionally.

Stir in cheese and serve. Make 8 cups (2 L).

Pictured on this page.

LINGUINI WITH RED CLAM SAUCE

Lots of tomato sauce with this instead of the more common light colored sauce.

Olive oil (or cooking oil)	3 tbsp.	50 mL
Chopped onion	1 cup	250 mL
Garlic cloves, minced	2	2
Canned tomatoes, with juice, broken up	28 oz.	796 mL
Granulated sugar	1 tsp.	5 mL
Salt	1 tsp.	5 mL
Pepper	¼ tsp.	1 mL
Ground oregano	½ tsp.	2 mL
Dried sweet basil	1 tsp.	5 mL
Tomato paste	5½ oz.	156 mL
Red wine (or alcohol-free wine)	½ cup	250 mL
Reserved clam juice		
Chopped parsley	1 tbsp.	15 mL
Baby clams, drained, juice reserved	2 × 5 oz.	2 × 142 g
Linguini	1 lb.	454 g
Boiling water	4 qts.	4 L
Cooking oil (optional)	1 tbsp.	15 mL
Salt	1 tbsp.	15 mL
Butter or hard margarine, melted	¼ cup	60 mL
Grated Parmesan cheese, for topping		

Heat olive oil in large saucepan. Add onion and garlic. Saute until soft.

Add next 10 ingredients. Stir together. Simmer, uncovered, for 10 minutes.

Add clams. Heat through.

Cook pasta in boiling water, cooking oil and second amount of salt in uncovered Dutch oven for 11 to 13 minutes until tender but firm. Drain.

Add melted butter and toss. Arrange pasta on 4 warmed plates.

Divide clam sauce over top of each serving. Sprinkle with cheese. Serves 4.

Pictured on page 43.

SMOKED SALMON PASTA

An extraordinary flavor. A family favorite.

Hard margarine (butter browns too fast)	2 tbsp.	30 mL
All-purpose flour	2 tbsp.	30 mL
Parsley flakes	½ tsp.	2 mL
Whole oregano, just a pinch		
Ground thyme, just a pinch		
Dried sweet basil, just a pinch		
Celery salt	¼ tsp.	1 mL
Chicken bouillon powder	1 tsp.	5 mL
Salt	½ tsp.	2 mL
Pepper	¼ tsp.	1 mL
Skim evaporated milk (or 1½ cups, 375 mL, whipping cream)	13½ oz.	385 mL
Commercial barbecued salmon, diced (about ½ lb., 225 g)	1⅓ cups	325 mL
Medium noodles	1 lb.	454 g
Boiling water	4 qts.	4 L
Cooking oil (optional)	1 tbsp.	15 mL
Salt	1 tbsp.	15 mL
Milk, if desired		

Melt margarine in saucepan. Mix in next 9 ingredients. Stir in milk until mixture boils and thickens.

Add salmon. Stir. Cover and keep warm.

Cook noodles in boiling water, cooking oil and salt in Dutch oven for 5 to 7 minutes until tender but firm. Drain. Return noodles to Dutch oven. Add salmon mixture. Toss. If you want it more moist, stir in a small amount of milk. Makes 8 cups (2 L).

Pictured on front cover.

PARÉ
pointer

Bakers usually go on strike because they want more dough.

PASTA WITH SHRIMP

This is a large attractive looking casserole.

Fettuccini, or other noodle pasta, broken in half	1 lb.	454 g
Hot water, to cover		
Tomatoes, peeled, seeded and diced (see Note)	4	4
Green onions, chopped	6	6
Dried oregano	1½ tsp.	7 mL
Canned shrimp, drained (or 1½ cups, 375 mL fresh, cooked)	2 × 4 oz.	2 × 113 g
Feta cheese, crumbled	½ lb.	225 g

Place pasta in 3 quart (3 L) casserole. Add hot water. Microwave, uncovered, on high (100%) power for about 15 minutes until tender but firm, stirring occasionally to keep from clumping. Drain.

Add tomatoes to pasta along with remaining 4 ingredients. Stir. Cover. Microwave on high (100%) power for about 5 minutes until hot through to bottom, stirring at half time. Serves 6.

Note: To peel tomatoes easily, dip into boiling water for about 1 minute.

Pictured below.

CHICKEN TETRAZZINI

Creamy chicken over fine noodles with a crispy-brown cheese topping.

Butter or hard margarine	3 tbsp.	50 mL
Chopped onion	1 cup	250 mL
Sliced fresh mushrooms	2 cups	500 mL
All-purpose flour	3 tbsp.	50 mL
Salt	½ tsp.	2 mL
Pepper	⅛ tsp.	0.5 mL
Nutmeg, just a pinch		
Chicken bouillon powder	1 tbsp.	15 mL
Water	2 cups	500 mL
Skim evaporated milk	1 cup	250 mL
Sherry (or alcohol-free sherry)	2 tbsp.	30 mL
Cubed cooked chicken	3 cups	750 mL
Vermicelli, or other noodle pasta, broken up	8 oz.	250 g
Boiling water	3 qts.	3 L
Cooking oil (optional)	1 tbsp.	15 mL
Salt	1 tbsp.	15 mL
Grated Parmesan cheese	½ cup	125 mL

Melt butter in frying pan. Add onion. Sauté for 3 to 4 minutes.

Add mushrooms. Sauté until onion is soft.

Mix in flour, salt, pepper, nutmeg and bouillon powder. Stir in water and milk until mixture boils and thickens.

Add sherry and chicken to sauce. Heat through.

Cook pasta in boiling water, cooking oil and salt in uncovered Dutch oven for 4 to 6 minutes until tender but firm. Drain. Add to chicken mixture. Turn into greased 3 quart (3 L) casserole.

Sprinkle with cheese. Bake, uncovered, in 350°F (175°C) oven for about 20 minutes until browned and hot. Serves 6 to 8.

PARÉ *pointer*

When he stood up to be counted, someone took his seat.

Pictured on page 43.

SPAGHETTI TIME

A full-bodied meat sauce covers a plateful of spaghetti. Add a salad for a complete meal.

TOMATO BEEF SAUCE

Lean ground beef	³/₄ lb.	340 g
Chopped onion	1 cup	250 mL
Chopped green pepper	¹/₃ cup	75 mL
Canned tomatoes, with juice, broken up	14 oz.	398 mL
Sliced fresh mushrooms	2 cups	500 mL
Grated carrot	¹/₂ cup	125 mL
Granulated sugar	¹/₂ tsp.	2 mL
White vinegar	2 tsp.	10 mL
Worcestershire sauce	1 tsp.	5 mL
Ground oregano	¹/₂ tsp.	2 mL
Dried sweet basil	¹/₂ tsp.	2 mL
Pepper	¹/₄ tsp.	1 mL
Frozen peas	1 cup	250 mL

SPAGHETTI

Spaghetti	8 oz.	250 g
Boiling water	3 qts.	3 L
Grated low-fat medium Cheddar cheese (less than 21% MF)	¹/₂ cup	125 mL

Tomato Beef Sauce: Sauté ground beef, onion and green pepper in non-stick frying pan until onion is soft and no pink remains in beef.

Add next 9 ingredients. Cover. Simmer slowly for about 15 minutes.

Add peas. Simmer for about 3 minutes to cook. Makes 4¹/₈ cups (1 L).

Spaghetti: Cook pasta in boiling water in uncovered Dutch oven for 11 to 13 minutes until tender but firm. Drain. Divide among 4 dinner plates. Spoon sauce over top.

Sprinkle with cheese. Makes 4 servings.

Pictured on this page.

These full-meal sandwich recipes are great for people on the go. They are loaded with meat, veggies and lots of extras. There are cold and hot varieties to choose from. The pizza-type sandwiches are really quick and the family will love them. Or try Spiced Chicken Buns, Tacos or Chicken Enchiladas if you want to add some "spice" to your life.

PITA LUNCH

This meaty sandwich uses leftover roast beef. A hearty lunch.

Thinly sliced lettuce, lightly packed	4½ cups	1.1 L
Shaved or chopped cooked roast beef	3 cups	750 mL
Grated medium Cheddar cheese	1½ cups	375 mL
Diced tomatoes	1½ cups	375 mL
Salad dressing (or mayonnaise)	6 tbsp.	100 mL
Prepared horseradish	¾ tsp.	4 mL
Prepared mustard	¾ tsp.	4 mL
Onion powder	¼ tsp.	1 mL
Salt, sprinkle		
Pepper, sprinkle		
Pita bread, halved crosswise	4	4

Place lettuce, roast beef, cheese and tomato in bowl. Add more cheese if desired.

Mix salad dressing, horseradish, mustard, onion powder, salt and pepper in small bowl. Pour over beef mixture. Toss.

Gently open pita along cut side. Divide filling among 8 pita "pockets". Serves 4.

TERIYAKI CHICKEN BURGERS

A grilled chicken breast makes a fine burger.

Soy sauce	¼ **cup**	**60 mL**
Brown sugar, packed	**2 tbsp.**	**30 mL**
Ground ginger	¼ **tsp.**	**1 mL**
Garlic powder	¼ **tsp.**	**1 mL**
Boneless, skinless large chicken breasts, halved	**3**	**3**
Canned pineapple slices, well drained	**6**	**6**
Lettuce leaves	**6**	**6**
Tomato slices	**6**	**6**
Salad dressing (or mayonnaise), as desired		
Hamburger buns, split and buttered	**6**	**6**

Combine soy sauce, brown sugar, ginger and garlic powder in small bowl. Stir.

Brush chicken with sauce. Cook on grill over medium heat for about 20 minutes total time. Turn and brush with sauce often.

Brush pineapple slices with sauce. Place on grill when chicken is almost cooked. Brown both sides.

Put lettuce, tomato, salad dressing, chicken and pineapple slice on bottom half of bun. Add top of bun. Makes 6 chicken burgers.

Pictured on this page.

SPICED CHICKEN BUNS

A special lunch to be sure.

Canned sliced peaches, with juice	14 oz.	398 mL
Brown sugar, packed	1/3 cup	75 mL
Lemon juice, fresh or bottled	1/2 tsp.	2 mL
Brandy flavoring	1/2 tsp.	2 mL
Ground cinnamon	1/8 tsp.	0.5 mL
Butter or hard margarine	1/4 cup	60 mL
All-purpose flour	1/4 cup	60 mL
Chicken bouillon powder	1 tsp.	5 mL
Salt	1/2 tsp.	2 mL
Paprika	1/4 tsp.	1 mL
Milk	2 cups	500 mL
Sherry (or alcohol-free sherry)	2 tbsp.	30 mL
Coarsely chopped cooked chicken	2 cups	500 mL
Ham slices, cut bun size at least 1/8 inch (3 mm) thick from cooked ham	12	12
Hamburger buns or English muffins, split, toasted and buttered	6	6

Put first 5 ingredients into small saucepan. Stir. Bring to a boil. Simmer for 5 minutes. Keep warm.

Melt butter in medium saucepan. Mix in flour, bouillon powder, salt and paprika. Stir in milk until mixture boils and thickens.

Add sherry and chicken. Return to a simmer.

Lay ham slices over top, overlapping. Cover. Simmer gently to warm ham.

Lay 2 bun halves on each of 6 plates. Using tongs, remove and place ham slice on each half. Spoon about 1/4 cup (60 mL) chicken sauce over each. Remove peach slices with slotted spoon and put on top of each bun half. Makes 6 servings of 2 bun halves each.

Pictured on page 61.

PARÉ
pointer

Unfortunately, when

a postman gets old

he loses his zip.

FISHBURGERS

These are fried in a pan rather than a deep-fryer. Made from canned salmon.

Butter or hard margarine	2 tsp.	10 mL
Chopped onion	1/3 cup	75 mL
Canned salmon, with liquid, skin and round bones removed	7 1/2 oz.	213 g
Large egg	1	1
Dry bread crumbs	1 1/2 cups	375 mL
Prepared mustard	1/2 tsp.	2 mL
Parsley flakes	1/4 tsp.	1 mL
Salt	1/4 tsp.	1 mL
Pepper, sprinkle		
Corn flakes crumbs	1/4 cup	60 mL
Butter or hard margarine	2 tbsp.	30 mL
TARTAR SAUCE		
Salad dressing (or mayonnaise)	2 tbsp.	30 mL
Sweet pickle relish	1 tsp.	5 mL
Hamburger buns, split and buttered	6	6

Melt first amount of butter in saucepan. Add onion and sauté until soft and clear. Remove from heat.

Mix in next 7 ingredients. Shape into 6 patties. If too dry, add another egg.

Dip patties into corn flakes crumbs. Melt second amount of butter in frying pan. Add fish patties. Brown both sides.

Tartar Sauce: Stir salad dressing and pickle relish together.

Spread tartar sauce on buns. Insert fish patties. Makes 6.

Pictured on page 55.

PARÉ *pointer*

The health clinic kept bandages in the refrigerator so they could use them for cold cuts.

BAKED CRAB SANDWICHES

Melted cheese with bacon—what could be better for a filler-upper?

Cream cheese, softened	4 oz.	125 g
Butter or hard margarine, softened	6 tbsp.	100 mL
Lemon juice, fresh or bottled	1 tsp.	5 mL
Worcestershire sauce	1/2 tsp.	2 mL
Onion powder	1/4 tsp.	1 mL
Crabmeat (or 1 can 4 oz., 113 g, drained), membrane removed	1 cup	250 mL
Hamburger buns or English muffins, split	5	5
Tomato slices	10	10
Yellow cheese slices	10	10
Bacon slices	10	10

Beat first 5 ingredients in small bowl until smooth.

Fold in crabmeat. Divide among bun halves. Spread.

Top with tomato slice, then cheese slice. Arrange on greased baking pan.

Fry bacon until crisp. Cut slices in half crosswise. Do not put bacon on buns yet. Bake buns in 350°F (175°C) oven for 8 to 10 minutes until cheese melts. Place 2 half slices of bacon on top of each bun to serve. Makes a generous 1 1/3 cups (325 mL) filling. Makes 10 bun halves, using 2 tbsp. (30 mL) each.

Pictured below.

Left: Fishburgers, page 54. Right: Baked Crab Sandwiches, page 55.

VEGETABLE PIZZA

Different from the usual pizza to be sure. Mild flavor with a good vegetable mixture.

CRUST

Biscuit mix	2 cups	500 mL
Milk	½ cup	125 mL

FILLING

Tomato sauce	7½ oz.	213 mL
Whole oregano	½ tsp.	2 mL
Dried sweet basil	½ tsp.	2 mL
Garlic powder	⅛ tsp.	0.5 mL
Granulated sugar	½ tsp.	2 mL
Finely chopped onion	¾ cup	175 mL
Broccoli florets	2 cups	500 mL
Sliced fresh mushrooms	1 cup	250 mL
Boiling water		
Grated mozzarella cheese	1 cup	250 mL
Canned whole baby corn, drained, halved	8	8
Grated mozzarella cheese	2 cups	500 mL

Crust: Stir biscuit mix with milk to form a ball. Knead on lightly floured surface 6 to 8 times. Press in greased 12 inch (30 cm) pizza pan.

Filling: Stir first 5 ingredients together. Spread over pizza crust.

Cook onion, broccoli and mushrooms in boiling water until tender crisp. Drain.

Sprinkle first amount of mozzarella cheese over sauce. Spoon cooked vegetables over top, then add corn. Sprinkle with remaining cheese. Bake on bottom rack in 425°F (220°C) oven for 12 to 15 minutes. Cuts into 8 wedges.

Pictured on this page.

SHRIMP SANDWICH

Elegant! Lots of shrimp.

Cream cheese, softened	4 oz.	125 g
Ripe avocado, peeled and mashed	1	1
Lemon juice, fresh or bottled	1 tsp.	5 mL
Salt	¼ tsp.	1 mL
Pepper, light sprinkle		
Garlic powder	⅛ tsp.	0.5 mL
Salad dressing (or mayonnaise)	½ cup	125 mL
Milk	2 tbsp.	30 mL
Lemon juice, fresh or bottled	2 tsp.	10 mL
Dill weed	¼ tsp.	1 mL
Cooked baby shrimp	1 lb.	454 g
Bread slices, toasted and buttered	8	8
Shredded lettuce, lightly packed	2 cups	500 mL
Cherry tomatoes, halved	4	4
Sprigs of fresh dill, for garnish	4	4

Beat first 6 ingredients together in bowl until smooth. Set aside.

Combine salad dressing, milk, lemon juice and dill weed in medium size bowl.

Fold in shrimp until coated.

Place 1 slice of toast on each large plate with bottom of slice facing you. Cut remaining slices in half diagonally. Place cut edges butting up against both sides of toast on plates.

Spread center slices with lettuce. Spoon avocado mixture over lettuce leaving edges showing. Divide shrimp over avocado.

Place tomato half at top and bottom of each plate. Garnish each with a sprig of dill. Serves 4.

PARÉ
pointer

Take your choice.

Would you rather

have laugh wrinkles

or worry warts?

MOCK PIZZA

Quick and easy. And a real hit!

English muffins, cut in half	6	6
Tomato sauce	7½ oz.	213 g
Dried sweet basil	¼ tsp.	1 mL
Ground oregano	¼ tsp.	1 mL
Onion powder	¼ tsp.	1 mL
Parsley flakes	¼ tsp.	1 mL
Seasoned salt	½ tsp.	2 mL
Grated mozzarella cheese	1 cup	250 mL
Cherry tomatoes, sliced	12	12
Small mushrooms, sliced	12	12
Bite-size pieces of pepperoni, ham, bacon or bologna	60	60
Grated mozzarella cheese	⅓ cup	75 mL

Arrange muffin halves on tray.

Stir next 6 ingredients together in small bowl. Spread over buns.

Layer next 4 ingredients over tomato sauce mixture in order given.

Sprinkle remaining cheese in center of each. Heat under broiler until hot and cheese is melted and bubbly. These may be prepared ahead and frozen before broiling. Makes 12 small pizzas.

Pictured above.

TACOS

A great do-it-yourself meal. Just fill your taco shell with layers.

Canned refried beans	14 oz.	398 mL
Salsa (mild, medium or hot)	1/4 cup	60 mL
Chopped iceberg lettuce	1 cup	250 mL
Tomato, diced	1	1
Red onion or other mild onion, cut in slivers (optional)	1	1
Grated mild or medium Cheddar cheese (or Monterey Jack cheese)	1/2 cup	125 mL
Sour cream (optional)	6 tbsp.	100 mL
Taco shells	8-10	8-10

Heat beans in heavy saucepan.

Place next 6 ingredients in separate containers ready to serve.

Divide beans among taco shells. Make additional layers of salsa, lettuce, tomato, onion, cheese and sour cream. Makes 10 tacos.

Pictured on front cover.

TIP

To save on preparation and clean up time during the week, grate 1/2 to 1 lb. (225 to 454 g) of your favorite hard cheese and store in a sealed plastic bag in refrigerator. Use within 2 weeks.

CHICKEN ENCHILADAS

This begins with a filling and ends with a pan full of wonderful enchiladas.

Cooking oil	2 tbsp.	30 mL
Boneless, skinless chicken breasts, diced	4	4
Chopped onion	1 cup	250 mL
Garlic clove, minced (or ¼ tsp., 1 mL, garlic powder)	1	1
Canned sliced mushrooms, drained	10 oz.	284 mL
Canned chopped green chilies, drained	4 oz.	114 mL
Sour cream	1 cup	250 mL
Chili powder	1 tsp.	5 mL
Ground cumin	1 tsp.	5 mL
Salt	½ tsp.	2 mL
Pepper	¼ tsp.	1 mL
Cooking oil	½ cup	125 mL
Corn tortillas	16	16
Grated medium Cheddar cheese or Monterey Jack cheese	2 cups	500 mL
TOPPING		
Sour cream	2 cups	500 mL
Grated medium Cheddar cheese or Monterey Jack cheese	2 cups	500 mL

Heat cooking oil in frying pan. Add chicken, onion and garlic. Stir-fry until no pink remains in chicken.

Stir next 7 ingredients together well in bowl. Add chicken mixture.

Heat second amount of cooking oil in frying pan. Using tongs, dip each tortilla into cooking oil to soften for 3 to 5 seconds per side. Add more cooking oil if needed. Drain on paper towels. Place scant ¼ cup (60 mL) chicken mixture in center of each tortilla. Add 2 tbsp. (30 mL) cheese. Roll tortilla tightly around filling. Arrange seam side down in 1 or 2 greased pans. Bake, uncovered, in 350°F (175°C) oven for 15 minutes until hot.

Topping: Spread sour cream over top. Sprinkle with cheese. Return to oven for about 5 minutes. Makes 16.

Pictured on page 63.

MUSHROOM BURGERS

Excellent texture, flavor and appearance. Good with or without cheese.

Large eggs	**2**	**2**
Finely chopped onion	**½ cup**	**125 mL**
Chopped fresh mushrooms	**2 cups**	**500 mL**
Fine dry bread crumbs	**½ cup**	**125 mL**
All-purpose flour	**¼ cup**	**60 mL**
Ground thyme	**¼ tsp.**	**1 mL**
Salt	**1 tsp.**	**5 mL**
Pepper	**¼ tsp.**	**1 mL**
Grated medium or sharp Cheddar cheese (optional)	**½ cup**	**125 mL**
Hamburger buns, split and buttered	**8**	**8**

Whisk eggs together in bowl. Stir in onion and mushrooms.

Add next 6 ingredients. Mix well. Shape into patties, using ¼ cup (60 mL) for each. Cook in greased frying pan, browning both sides.

Insert patties into buns. Serve with condiments. Makes 8 burgers.

Pictured below.

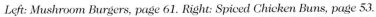

Left: Mushroom Burgers, page 61. Right: Spiced Chicken Buns, page 53.

PIZZA BREAD

A quick lunch. Just cut a French loaf in half, spread with pizza makings and bake.

French bread loaf, sliced lengthwise, buttered	1	1
Tomato paste	5½ oz.	156 mL
Grated Parmesan cheese	3 tbsp.	50 mL
Dried sweet basil	½ tsp.	2 mL
Whole oregano	½ tsp.	2 mL
Garlic powder	¼ tsp.	1 mL
Grated mozzarella cheese	2 cups	500 mL
Sliced pepperoni or other cooked meat	1¼ cups	300 mL
Sliced fresh mushrooms	2 cups	500 mL
Small green pepper, diced	1	1
Grated mozzarella cheese	1 cup	250 mL
Grated medium Cheddar cheese	½ cup	125 mL

Arrange bread halves on tray, buttered side up. Broil until toasty brown.

Mix next 5 ingredients in small bowl. Spread over bread.

Sprinkle with first amount of mozzarella cheese, followed by pepperoni, mushrooms and green pepper. Place on baking tray.

Scatter second amount of mozzarella cheese lengthwise over top. Sprinkle Cheddar cheese down center of each bread half. Bake in 450°F (230°C) oven until hot and cheese is melted. Cut each bread half crosswise into 2 to 3 inch (5 to 7.5 cm) slices. Serves 4.

Pictured on page 63.

Clockwise from top left: Chicken Enchiladas, page 60; Garbanzo Soup, page 65; and Pizza Bread, page 62.

These hearty soups are deliciously filling and make a wonderful meal on a cold day. Serve with your favorite type of bun and your meal is complete. The variety of creamy chowders, wholesome bean and broth-based soups will be enjoyed at any lunch or dinner.

BLACK BEAN SOUP

Soup at its darkest. Mild and tasty. Easy to double or triple recipe.

Water	1½ cups	375 mL
Canned black beans, with liquid	19 oz.	540 mL
Instant vegetable stock mix	4 tsp.	20 mL
Ground coriander	¼ tsp.	1 mL
Ground cumin	¼ tsp.	1 mL
Sweet pickle relish	1 tsp.	5 mL
Hot pepper sauce (add more if desired)	¼ tsp.	1 mL
Sour cream	2 tbsp.	30 mL
Grated Monterey Jack cheese	2 tsp.	10 mL

Run water and beans through blender. Pour into saucepan.

Add next 5 ingredients. Stir. Heat, stirring often, as mixture comes to a boil. Boil slowly, uncovered, for about 10 minutes to blend flavors.

Pour into 2 bowls. Top each with 1 tbsp. (15 mL) sour cream. Sprinkle each with 1 tsp. (5 mL) cheese. Makes 2 cups (500 mL).

GARBANZO SOUP

This has its own good flavor. Great choice.

Cooking oil	2 tbsp.	30 mL
Chopped onion	1½ cups	375 mL
Canned tomatoes, with juice, broken up	14 oz.	398 mL
Ketchup	2 tbsp.	30 mL
Instant vegetable stock mix	2 tbsp.	30 mL
Whole oregano	1 tsp.	5 mL
Garlic powder	¼ tsp.	1 mL
Salt	½ tsp.	2 mL
Pepper	⅛ tsp.	0.5 mL
Cayenne pepper	⅛ tsp.	0.5 mL
Water	3 cups	750 mL
Garbanzo beans (chick peas), with liquid, puréed in blender	19 oz.	540 mL
Plain yogurt or sour cream, per serving	1 tbsp.	15 mL

Heat cooking oil in large saucepan. Add onion. Sauté until soft.

Add next 9 ingredients. Heat, stirring often, until mixture comes to a boil. Boil gently for 15 minutes.

Add garbanzo purée. Stir. Return to a boil. Boil slowly for about 10 minutes to blend flavors well. Divide between 2 to 4 soup bowls.

Add yogurt to center of each bowl. Makes 6 cups (1.5 L).

Pictured on page 63.

TIP

A blender or food processor is a handy time-saver for quick chopping of vegetables to be used in soups. Some of the recipes also require a blender or processor to pureé the cooked veggies or beans.

EASY SALMON CHOWDER

A thick and full chowder.

Bacon slices, cut in small pieces	3	3
Chopped onion	1 cup	250 mL
Thinly sliced or diced carrot	¾ cup	175 mL
Chopped celery	¾ cup	175 mL
Water	½ cup	125 mL
Condensed cream of potato soup	2 × 10 oz.	2 × 284 mL
Skim evaporated milk (or light cream)	13½ oz.	385 mL
Salt	¼ tsp.	1 mL
Pepper	⅛ tsp.	0.5 mL
Canned salmon, with liquid	7½ oz.	213 g

Fry bacon and onion slowly in heavy Dutch oven until clear and soft.

Add carrot, celery and water. Cover. Simmer until tender.

Add potato soup, milk, salt and pepper. Stir.

Remove skin and round bones from salmon. Flake. Add salmon and liquid to Dutch oven. Heat slowly, stirring often, until steaming hot but not boiling. Makes 6⅓ cups (1.6 L).

Pictured below.

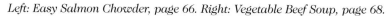

Left: Easy Salmon Chowder, page 66. Right: Vegetable Beef Soup, page 68.

CHEESY HAM CHOWDER

The addition of peas to blended vegetables gives a distinctive flavor. A fabulous chowder.

Diced potato	2 cups	500 mL
Diced onion	1 cup	250 mL
Diced carrot	1/3 cup	75 mL
Chicken bouillon cube (1/4 oz., 6 g, size)	1	1
Water	1 cup	250 mL
Parsley flakes	1 tsp.	5 mL
Peas, fresh or frozen	3/4 cup	175 mL
Canned flaked ham	6 1/2 oz.	184 g
Milk	2 cups	500 mL
Mild processed cheese (such as Velveeta), cut up	8 oz.	250 g

Put first 6 ingredients into saucepan. Simmer until vegetables are tender. Cool a bit, then process in blender. Transfer back into saucepan.

Add peas, ham, milk and cheese. Heat, stirring often. Gently simmer to cook peas and melt cheese. Makes about 8 cups (2 L).

QUICK MINESTRONE

A tasty shortcut to a well-known soup.

Condensed chicken noodle soup	10 oz.	284 mL
Condensed vegetable soup	10 oz.	284 mL
Water	1 1/4 cups	300 mL
Canned kidney beans, with liquid	14 oz.	398 mL
Chopped cooked roast beef (or 1/4 lb., 113 g, scramble-fried ground beef)		

Put all 5 ingredients into saucepan. Bring to a boil. Simmer for a few minutes to allow flavors to blend. Makes about 5 cups (1.25 L).

PARÉ
pointer

He heard that hard work never killed anybody but he's not taking any chances.

VEGETABLE BEEF SOUP

Definitely a meal in itself. A very filling soup.

Cooking oil	2 tsp.	10 mL
Lean ground beef	½ lb.	225 g
Canned tomatoes, with juice, broken up	14 oz.	398 mL
Frozen mixed vegetables	10 oz.	284 g
Peeled and diced onion	1 cup	250 mL
Water	4 cups	1 L
Beef bouillon powder	1 tbsp.	15 mL
Ground thyme	¼ tsp.	1 mL
Salt	1 tsp.	5 mL
Pepper	¼ tsp.	1 mL

Place cooking oil and ground beef in large saucepan over medium heat. Scramble-fry ground beef until browned and crumbly and no pink remains.

Add remaining 8 ingredients. Stir. Bring to a boil. Cover. Boil slowly, turning down heat as needed. Simmer for about 20 minutes until vegetables are tender. Serve with crackers or crusty rolls. Makes about 8½ cups (2.1 L).

Pictured on page 66.

PARÉ
pointer

Those two are just

like blisters. They

show up when the

work is finished.

Once the vegetables are chopped, stir-frys take no time at all. Use a food processor to cut down on the chopping time. Have family members or casual guests help prepare the vegetables to make time go by even faster. Purchase a non-stick wok or bowl-type frying pan and eliminate the oil from those recipes.

STIR-FRY MEAL

A quick meal with a good flavor. Do on the barbecue or on the stove.

Cooking oil	3 tbsp.	50 mL
Sirloin steak, cut in very thin slices	1 lb.	454 g
Sliced fresh mushrooms	2 cups	500 mL
Sliced onion	2 cups	500 mL
Sliced celery	2 cups	500 mL
Green onions, sliced	10-12	10-12
Canned bamboo shoots, drained and cut in matchsticks	10 oz.	284 mL
Small red pepper, cut in matchsticks	1	1
Canned spinach, drained and chopped	1/2 cup	125 mL
Soy sauce	1/4 cup	60 mL
Granulated sugar	2 tsp.	10 mL
Beef bouillon powder	1 tsp.	5 mL
Hot water	1/2 cup	125 mL

Heat cooking oil in wok or large skillet on grill over medium heat. Add steak pieces. Sauté until browned.

Add next 6 ingredients. Stir. Cover. Cook for 5 minutes.

Add spinach, soy sauce and sugar. Stir.

Dissolve bouillon powder in hot water. Add to vegetable mixture. Stir-fry for 10 to 15 minutes until tender. Makes 3 servings.

Pictured on page 73.

PORK STIR-FRY

A good colorful stir-fry. Fresh tomatoes give this low-fat meal a real lift.

Cooking oil	1 tsp.	5 mL
Thinly sliced celery	1 cup	250 mL
Green onions, sliced	2	2
Coarsely chopped bok choy or cabbage	3 cups	750 mL
Water	¼ cup	60 mL
Cooking oil	1 tbsp.	15 mL
Lean pork steak, cut in thin strips, all visible fat removed (see Note)	1 lb.	454 g
Cornstarch	2 tsp.	10 mL
Beef bouillon packet (35% less salt)	1 × ¼ oz.	1 × 6.5 g
Water	½ cup	125 mL
Light soy sauce (40% less salt)	1 tbsp.	15 mL
Garlic powder	¼ tsp.	1 mL
Ground ginger	¼ tsp.	1 mL
Medium tomatoes, cut bite size	3	3
Fresh spinach or dark green lettuce, cut in strips, packed	1 cup	250 mL
Canned whole baby corn, cut in ½ inch (12 mm) pieces	½ cup	125 mL

Heat first amount of cooking oil in wok or frying pan. Add celery, onion and bok choy. Stir-fry for about 1 minute.

Add first amount of water. Cover. Simmer for 5 to 7 minutes until tender. Remove to bowl.

Heat second amount of cooking oil in wok. Add pork strips. Stir-fry for about 15 minutes until browned and no pink remains.

Mix next 6 ingredients in small bowl. Add to pork. Stir until mixture boils and thickens. Add cooked vegetables. Heat and stir.

Add tomatoes, spinach and corn. Cover. Allow to heat through for about 1 minute. Makes 4 servings.

Note: It is easier to thinly cut meat when it is partially frozen.

Pictured on page 73.

STIR-FRY MEAL

Simply delectable! Easily doubled. Less sodium in this version.

Cooking oil	1 tbsp.	15 mL
Boneless, skinless chicken breast, halved	1	1
Bok choy or suey choy, torn up, packed	1 cup	250 mL
Sliced fresh mushrooms	1 cup	250 mL
Broccoli florets, cut small	1 cup	250 mL
Fresh bean sprouts	1 cup	250 mL
Grated carrot	1 cup	250 mL
Red or green pepper, slivered	1	1
Frozen whole pea pods (or fresh)	6 oz.	170 g
Water	3 tbsp.	50 mL
Light soy sauce (40% less salt)	¼ cup	60 mL
Cornstarch	1 tsp.	5 mL
Ground ginger	⅛ tsp.	0.5 mL
Garlic powder	⅛ tsp.	0.5 mL
Pepper	¼ tsp.	1 mL

Heat cooking oil in wok or frying pan. Cut chicken into small pieces. Add chicken to wok or frying pan. Stir-fry until no pink remains. Transfer chicken to bowl.

Add next 7 ingredients to wok. Stir-fry for about 3 minutes.

Add water. Stir in chicken. Cover and simmer for about 7 minutes until cooked.

Mix remaining 5 ingredients in small cup. Stir into vegetable mixture. Stir-fry to mix and thicken. Makes 2 servings.

TIP

If you will be using oil to cook with in a wok or frying pan, first heat the pan until droplets of water shaken onto the surface bounce and "dance". Add the oil. This will prevent the oil from heating too hot and possibly igniting.

CHICKEN VEGETABLE FRY

Serve this stir-fry with steamed rice to round off the meal.

Cooking oil	2 tbsp.	30 mL
Water	2 tbsp.	30 mL
Red wine vinegar	2½ tbsp.	37 mL
Whole oregano	½ tsp.	2 mL
Garlic powder	⅛ tsp.	0.5 mL
Salt	¼ tsp.	1 mL
Small short thin carrot sticks	1 cup	250 mL
Boneless, skinless chicken breast, halved, cut bite size	1	1
Broccoli florets	1 cup	250 mL
Cauliflower florets	1 cup	250 mL
Sliced green onion	⅓ cup	75 mL
Soy sauce	4 tsp.	20 mL
Cornstarch	¼ tsp.	1 mL
Ground ginger	½ tsp.	2 mL

Combine first 6 ingredients in wok or frying pan.

Add carrot sticks. Stir-fry on medium-high for about 4 minutes until tender crisp.

Add chicken. Stir-fry for 3 to 4 minutes until no pink remains.

Add broccoli, cauliflower and onion. Stir. Cover. Cook on low, stirring occasionally, for 5 minutes.

Mix remaining 3 ingredients in small cup. Add, stirring until mixture bubbles. Serves 2.

PARÉ
pointer

They don't mind

suffering in silence

just as long as

everybody knows it.

Clockwise from top left: Walnut Chicken Stir-Fry, page 74; Pork Stir-Fry, page 70; and Stir-Fry Meal, page 69.

WALNUT CHICKEN STIR-FRY

Colorful, nutty, chewy, crispy. Great treat.

Cooking oil	2 tbsp.	30 mL
Chopped onion	1½ cups	375 mL
Thinly sliced celery	1½ cups	375 mL
Small red pepper, slivered	1	1
Cooking oil	2 tbsp.	30 mL
Boneless, skinless chicken breasts, slivered	2	2
Chopped walnuts	1 cup	250 mL
Slivered Chinese cabbage	3 cups	750 mL
Canned sliced water chestnuts, drained	10 oz.	284 mL
Canned bamboo shoots, drained and sliced	10 oz.	284 mL
Soy sauce	3 tbsp.	50 mL
Sherry (or alcohol-free sherry)	2 tbsp.	30 mL
Granulated sugar	1 tsp.	5 mL
Garlic powder	¼ tsp.	1 mL
Ground ginger	¼ tsp.	1 mL
Salt	½ tsp.	2 mL
Cornstarch	4 tsp.	20 mL
Water	¼ cup	60 mL

Heat first amount of cooking oil in wok or frying pan. Add onion, celery and red pepper. Stir-fry until soft. Turn into bowl.

Add second amount of cooking oil to wok. Add chicken. Stir-fry until no pink remains.

Add walnuts and cabbage. Stir-fry for 4 minutes to wilt cabbage.

Add next 8 ingredients along with onion mixture. Stir-fry for 5 minutes.

Mix cornstarch with water in small cup. Add and stir until thickened and glazed. Makes 6½ cups (1.6 L).

Pictured on page 73.

PARÉ
pointer

With so many rocks

in its bed, the sea is

bound to be restless.

CHICKEN STIR-FRY

As everyone is sitting around you can whip up this stir-fry on the barbecue. Serve with rice.

Cooking oil	2 tbsp.	30 mL
Chicken or pork, cut in small cubes	l lb.	454 g
Large onion, chopped	1	1
Fresh bean sprouts	12 oz.	350 g
Thinly sliced celery	2 cups	500 mL
Canned bamboo shoots, drained and sliced	8 oz.	227 mL
Soy sauce	1 tbsp.	15 mL
Garlic powder	⅛ tsp.	0.5 mL
Salt	¼ tsp.	1 mL
Pepper	¼ tsp.	1 mL
Beef bouillon powder	2 tsp.	10 mL
Hot water	1 cup	250 mL
Cornstarch	1 tbsp.	15 mL
Cold water	1 tbsp.	15 mL

Heat cooking oil in wok or large skillet over hot grill. Add chicken. Stir-fry for 5 minutes.

Add next 8 ingredients. Stir-fry until chicken is no longer pink and vegetables are tender crisp.

Dissolve beef bouillon in hot water. Add to wok. Stir.

Mix cornstarch in cold water. Add to wok, stirring until mixture cooks and thickens. Taste for pepper, adding more as desired. Makes 4 servings.

Pictured on this page.

CHICKEN STIR-FRY

Serve this colorful dish with noodles or rice for a full meal.

Cooking oil	2 tbsp.	30 mL
Boneless, skinless chicken breasts, halved, slivered or cubed	2	2
Medium onion, sliced in thin rings	1	1
Thinly sliced carrot coins	1 cup	250 mL
Thinly sliced celery	½ cup	125 mL
Coarsely chopped fresh mushrooms	1 cup	250 mL
Medium zucchini, with peel, slivered or cubed	2	2
Water	2 tbsp.	30 mL
Snow peas, fresh or frozen, thawed	6 oz.	170 g
Green pepper, slivered	1	1
Freshly grated ginger (or ¼ tsp., 1 mL, ground)	1 tsp.	5 mL
Green onions, sliced	2-3	2-3
Cornstarch	2 tsp.	10 mL
Soy sauce	2 tsp.	10 mL
Sherry (or alcohol-free sherry)	2 tbsp.	30 mL
Cayenne pepper	⅛ tsp.	0.5 mL
Salt	½ tsp.	2 mL

Heat cooking oil in wok or large frying pan. Add chicken. Stir-fry until no pink remains. Turn into bowl.

Add next 6 ingredients to wok. Cover. Steam for about 5 minutes until tender crisp.

Add snow peas, green pepper, ginger and onion. Stir-fry for about 5 minutes to soften. Add chicken. Heat through.

Mix cornstarch, soy sauce, sherry, cayenne pepper, and salt. Stir into wok contents to thicken and coat. Makes 6½ cups (1.6 L).

Pictured on front cover.

P A R É
pointer

It is easy to joke

with a fish. They fall

for it hook, line and

sinker.

Measurement Tables

Throughout this book measurements are given in Conventional and Metric measure. To compensate for differences between the two measurements due to rounding, a full metric measure is not always used. The cup used is the standard 8 fluid ounce. Temperature is given in degrees Fahrenheit and Celsius. Baking pan measurements are in inches and centimetres as well as quarts and litres. An exact metric conversion is given below as well as the working equivalent (Standard Measure).

OVEN TEMPERATURES

Fahrenheit (°F)	Celsius (°C)
175°	80°
200°	95°
225°	110°
250°	120°
275°	140°
300°	150°
325°	160°
350°	175°
375°	190°
400°	205°
425°	220°
450°	230°
475°	240°
500°	260°

SPOONS

Conventional Measure	Metric Exact Conversion Millilitre (mL)	Metric Standard Measure Millilitre (mL)
$1/8$ teaspoon (tsp.)	0.6 mL	0.5 mL
$1/4$ teaspoon (tsp.)	1.2 mL	1 mL
$1/2$ teaspoon (tsp.)	2.4 mL	2 mL
1 teaspoon (tsp.)	4.7 mL	5 mL
2 teaspoons (tsp.)	9.4 mL	10 mL
1 tablespoon (tbsp.)	14.2 mL	15 mL

CUPS

	Metric Exact Conversion	Metric Standard Measure
$1/4$ cup (4 tbsp.)	56.8 mL	60 mL
$1/3$ cup ($5 1/3$ tbsp.)	75.6 mL	75 mL
$1/2$ cup (8 tbsp.)	113.7 mL	125 mL
$2/3$ cup ($10 2/3$ tbsp.)	151.2 mL	150 mL
$3/4$ cup (12 tbsp.)	170.5 mL	175 mL
1 cup (16 tbsp.)	227.3 mL	250 mL
$4 1/2$ cups	1022.9 mL	1000 mL (1 L)

PANS

Conventional Inches	Metric Centimetres
8x8 inch	20x20 cm
9x9 inch	22x22 cm
9x13 inch	22x33 cm
10x15 inch	25x38 cm
11x17 inch	28x43 cm
8x2 inch round	20x5 cm
9x2 inch round	22x5 cm
$10x4 1/2$ inch tube	25x11 cm
8x4x3 inch loaf	20x10x7 cm
9x5x3 inch loaf	22x12x7 cm

DRY MEASUREMENTS

Conventional Measure Ounces (oz.)	Metric Exact Conversion Grams (g)	Metric Standard Measure Grams (g)
1 oz.	28.3 g	30 g
2 oz.	56.7 g	55 g
3 oz.	85.0 g	85 g
4 oz.	113.4 g	125 g
5 oz.	141.7 g	140 g
6 oz.	170.1 g	170 g
7 oz.	198.4 g	200 g
8 oz.	226.8 g	250 g
16 oz.	453.6 g	500 g
32 oz.	907.2 g	1000 g (1 kg)

CASSEROLES (CANADA & BRITAIN)

Standard Size Casserole	Exact Metric Measure
1 qt. (5 cups)	1.13 L
$1 1/2$ qts. ($7 1/2$ cups)	1.69 L
2 qts. (10 cups)	2.25 L
$2 1/2$ qts. ($12 1/2$ cups)	2.81 L
3 qts. (15 cups)	3.38 L
4 qts. (20 cups)	4.5 L
5 qts. (25 cups)	5.63 L

CASSEROLES (UNITED STATES)

Standard Size Casserole	Exact Metric Measure
1 qt. (4 cups)	900 mL
$1 1/2$ qts. (6 cups)	1.35 L
2 qts. (8 cups)	1.8 L
$2 1/2$ qts. (10 cups)	2.25 L
3 qts. (12 cups)	2.7 L
4 qts. (16 cups)	3.6 L
5 qts. (20 cups)	4.5 L

Index

COOKBOOKS

Chicken Greens Salad, page 32.

Company's Coming cookbooks are available at retail locations everywhere.

For information contact:

COMPANY'S COMING PUBLISHING LIMITED

Box 8037, Station "F"	Box 17870
Edmonton, Alberta	San Diego, California
Canada T6H 4N9	U.S.A. 92177-7870

TEL: (403) 450-6223
FAX: (403) 450-1857